THE BEGGARS'SONG

Pious Okoro

Gwendolyn Brooks Poetry Prize-winning Author

Publisher's information, address:

Cissus World Press, P.O. Box 240865, Milwaukee, WI 53224

www.cissusworldpressbooks.com

First published in the U.S.A by Cissus World Press

ISBN: 978-0-9679511-8-8

Cover Design: Dike Okoro
Cover Art: Pious Okoro

CISSUS WORLD PRESS books are published by Dike Okoro, Founding Publisher.

Note from the author:

The Beggars' Songs, Pious Okoro's second collection of poetry, affirms him as a poet of lively, simple, and yet serious purpose. The poems are divided in sections titled: *Season of Corruption, War Songs, Alone with her God, Oil Songs, The Broken Pieces Fall in Place,* and *Telling Tall Tales.* In this volume, Okoro gives corruption a face using a mature poetic voice that addresses provocative themes and captures experiences that readers can enjoy and relate with in our age of one global village. Additionally, the poet takes an excursion into complex human experiences such as war, grief, death, childhood, tragedy, triumphs, oil and the brutal power play associated with post-independence Nigerian/African politics.

To the memory of
CLARA OKECHUKWU OKORO
my mother

In the beginning was the Word, and the Word

was with God, and the Word was God. -John 1:1

Contents

TELLING TALL TALES

SEASON OF CORRUPTION

GANG OF LOITERS AND LOOTERS

Sons and daughters without shame
No different from their fathers
Who were booed and booted
Out of office in the homeland

Their names charm the people
They hide under this lie to loiter
 All season in the corridor of power
An albatross of a divided house

They swim in mucky waters
No different from political ducks
That shake their plumage dry, as
Their crooked feet touch the ground

Loiters and looters whose
Season of grabbing never ends
Booing and booting will not do it
Shamefully they are our face

THE BEGGARS' SONG

The hands of beggars
Greet you at every turn
Like pinchers raised in the air
You cannot ignore them
And crab-like their feet move
A little budge to the left
And to the right as they sight
Approaching prey

They start their prowling day
As men and women of honor
But at the road check points
Other duty posts and marts
They trade the honor
Of uniform for a morsel
Of bread, as they sing
The beggars' song with a smile

Like smog that covers the land
The beggar's sway
Is here to stay
For the same hands that gather
Also hides behind the feather
Of uniform to mock the law
Like hearing the voice of Jacob
But the man is Esau

THE PEOPLE'S HOUSE

At the people's house
Seating yes men and women
Nap at the people's expense

Chattering weaver birds
Waste their days singing
To the deaf in the courtyard

For the honorables know
With night comes mocking
Of the waiting crickets

So, they defiantly sleep
Unruffled to the ominous cry
Of the night owl

Disturbingly, the mosquitoes
Whisper in their ears, 'good night'
Without stinging them

FOLLOW THE MONEY

Follow the money
The trail is there
From tree to tree
Follow its flight to the West
And you have a caged bird

Follow the money
Follow the raised dust
See the vultures fight
Plucking feathers
Positioning themselves to loot

Follow the money
Looting is the culture
Lost is the future
The resilient voice
And will to pick stones

YESTERDAY SPEAKS TODAY

Yesterday speaks today
See the bloody hands
See the inglorious generals
Donning 'bloody civilian' clothes
And beating their chest like gorillas

These chameleons speak
All the languages of sham
They stand in the village square
Soliciting shameless political harlots
Under the probing sun

In this season of shame
They charm scandalous choirs
Like fire flies to death dance
Singing from their contemptible pockets
Songs peppered with pretence

THEY KILLED THE FISHERMAN
(For PW)

The fisherman's song
Was a reminder of the riotous
Days of Kalakula republic
The police responded swiftly
To contain street touts
Who may want to dance

The damning song
Did not spare the band
Of elected robbers
Who loot the people's treasury
While, our watch dogs
Look the other way

The fisherman's song
Was as direct as a good shot
"They killed the fisherman"
His lone voice was heard
Crying in the streets
Of Yenagoa

* **Yenagoa** – Capital of Beyelsa state (Nigeria)

ECHOES OF BRUTALITY
(At Apapa Bus stop)

He grabbed the lad's neck
Like the handle of a hammer
And repeatedly slammed his head
Against the body of the motionless bus
'Owo da,' he screamed into his ear
With each slamming of the head

Under the watchful Lagosians' eyes
That included the free riding soldiers
And the other passengers
Who daily are fed such public specter
'Owo da,' he screamed into his ear
With each slamming of the head

Sustained pounding of hard rocks
Yield result; as the kid was broken
The delayed fare was produced
Years after witnessing that show of shame
'Owo da,' still echoes in my head
And, I am not sure who to blame

Owo ada (*Yoruba language for "Where is the money?"*); **Apapa** (*a precinct of Lagos, Nigeria*)

17

CATCH AND RELEASE GAME

Elephants are on rampage
Rumbling, stomping and plundering
Away all that makes us a great land
In this season of corruption

Rats are tracked and trapped
For a morsel
While the troubling elephants
Are caught and released

While the police tamper arrest
Judges pamper justice
Only in the West are our elephants
Caged like canary to sing

FACE TO FACE WITH KILLERS
(*For Bola Ige*)

If walls could but speak
They will cry out, betrayal
Of the enemy in the house
If the peoples' justice minister
With security operatives swarming
Around him like bees, could be
Murdered, like plucking a mango
Off the tree

If walls could but speak
They will cry out, betrayal
As his official security disappeared
Like weaver birds do upon sighting
A snake in their nestling abode
Where they mate and make love songs
Face to face with hired killers
Oga was alone, like most Nigerians
Are abandoned to watch
Their own back

*Oga (*Pidgin english, for; boss*)
* Bola Ige (*Assassinated Nigerian Attorney General for Justice*)

19

SEASON OF CORRUPTION

The once commanding rooster
Retires to a coop
Not to a lavish hilltop
Pen, standing out in a shanty sea
But the mocking birds
Would give him no rest
Yesterday, they sang his praise
When he accepted the call

An invitation
'To come and eat'

The crowned young roosters
With plumage authority
Out in the field
Are compelled to roost
For not playing
The street hawk
That must forage all day
For returns to the office

Monkey dey work
Baboon dey wack

While the roosters that once
Walked with their wings down

Clucking like distressed hen
Robbed of her chicks
Saintly call those in power
Corrupt to their faces
But with wind of change
A new song is born

'It's our time to eat'

Monkey dey work baboon dey wack (English language translation:
one fellow labors while another eats)
While Chop (pidgin english word for Eat).

PASSING THE NEEDLE'S EYE

Give the police kola nut
At the road check point
His face shines as moon
And he blesses you
Like a fake priest in the land

Give him nothing
His eyes turn red like pepper
Pray you do not see pepper
He employs delay ploy
Like the spider's web
That traps and stops the fly

Like passing the needle's eye
The highways are death traps
Riddled with pot- holes
Sure gateway to the grave
Escape them, the police
Green pasture awaits you

- **Kola nut** (pidgin english for bribe money)

WHEN WILL ENOUGH BE ENOUGH?

When will enough be enough?
Unending political thieves line up
Like birds on street power wires
Daring boys to pull the catapult

When will enough be enough?
The people are trampled upon again
And again like fallen dry leaves
Their voice ignored by the crushing feet

When will enough be enough?
Which voice will wake the Jonahs?
The voice of thunder, or barking
Of toothless dogs in the wild dog world

WHAT THE EMPEROR DID NOT SEE

When the paid praise singers
Like a choir of mosquitoes
Come singing
Their unsolicited songs
The people in amazement
Clap hands not in amusement
For the sake of their belly

And the man being praised
Declares himself the emperor
When the ear can no longer
Tell the cricket's lullaby
From the monkey's warning calls
There must be something
The emperor is not seeing

FATE OF THE SHEEP

Corruption once sat at the corridor
While men wined, she came into the parlor
As men slept, she crept into the bedroom
Leaving no space to spare in the house

Our home now breeds corruption
Fostered by the people for the people
Festered by the people for the people
Leaving every man to be eaten by a bigger game

The order now is by brute canine power
Frightening is the fate of the sheep that has no horn
Living in the midst of the wild dogs
Leaving little room for the survival of her kind

DOUBLE TROUBLE

Our front door to the world
The Murtala Airport
Built to stand shoulder to shoulder
With the Heathrow and J. F. Kennedy airports
But she stoops to challenges
And gives the wayfarer headache
He would rather pray not to experience

At the airport, pan handlers
Dressed in uniform walk you
Through the screening maze
Like the screaming maze
Of Jankara mart
Invoking seed of unease
That hangs in the air

Snooping eyes like the sun
Surely observed the play
By the uniform locals
For before boarding the big bird
The foreign airlines screen again
Snapping the screening charade
With one of their own

As the big bird takes to air
And gets swallowed up

By the night cloud
My eyes close with mixed feelings
Saddened…
Alien hands screen better
While we scream better
Even, in our front door

January 9, 2014

Murtala Airport(abridged for Murtala Mohammed International Airport, Lagos)
Jankara market is the largest market in Lagos.

SONGBIRDS OF THE LAND
(For MKO, Saro, Fela, Gani, and Tai)

The seasons wait for no man
While we remain mere bird watchers

For songbirds have their seasons
To sing, and they are gone

MKO defied the political odds
To perch on the iroko and got killed

Saro sang loudly of the polluted land
To be heard by all, and got killed

Fela struck a chord with the people
In their turbulent seasons, and flew off

Gani with an eagle's keen vision
Flew away with the season beyond reach

Tai perched on the mayflower singing
Refused bribe in his season, before flying away

MKO (M.K.O. Abiola: A philanthropic business man, and the people's choice in Nigeria's 1993 presidential election that was annulled by the military).

Saro (Ken Saro- Wiwa: Nigerian writer and environmental activist who was outspoken critic of the government's coziness with the foreign petroleum companies operating in the Niger Delta).
Fela (Fela Anikulaapo- Kuti: Nigeria musician, human rights activist, and political activist).
Gani (Gani Fawehinmi: Nigerian civil right lawyer, Senior Advocate of Nigeria, and author).
Tai :(Nigerian educator, and social activist).

WAR SONGS

OUTNUMBERED AT THE TABLE
(For Major Isaac Adaka Boro)

In defense of the Niger Delta
His rag-tag army gallantly took arms
Giving the creek boys a voice

In defense of one Nigeria
He donned Fed uniforms, took arms
And paid with his blood

In defense of the dying dream
The creek is still restive
Outnumbered at the table

31

THE CHILD AT WAR TIME

The war came to an end
Opening the door for peace
But, as the military stretched its tentacles
To seek and take any moving likeness
Of the vanquished male tribe
That once stood their ground
Against the mighty army

The end song was a mirage
Men disappeared like praire dogs
As soldiers sniffed and snatched
Suspected enemies of the state
From house to house raid
Under the cover of night

Soldiers stormed our house
Unannounced before dawn
Led by an Idi Amin look-alike
Who in his mad parade
As the OC fired a shot at me
"Dis one na carbon copy"

A child at war time
Whose papa, they came
To whisk away
To face the Adekunle's trial*

Thank God
Pa returned alive to tell his story

* **Adekunle's trial**: A military court headed by Col. Benjamin Adekunle in Port Harcourt at the end of the Nigeria / Biafra war, that tried cases of people suspected or alleged to have aided the Biafran course.

AN UNDYING VOICE
(*For Gen. Mamman J. Vatsa*)

He went to war
In jack-boots
No books
Rifle bearing
But, the muse
Conscripted him

Boots on the ground
Gboooom...ta... ta…
Rang in the air
Saturday at Ikok*
His voice boomed
With a new song

Evening
Even at war time
The soldier
Remained a poet
An undying
Voice

*Gen. Mamman J. Vatsa(*Nigerian Army Major General and poet, who was executed in 1986 for an alleged coup plot against Gen. Ibrahim Babangida.)*
*Ikok *(a town in Cross River State, Nigeria, close to the Cameroon border)*
*Saturday at Ikok *(a poem written by Mamman J. Vatsa)*

THEY KILLED OUR SONG

The sight of the homing women
From farm with loaded basins
Sitting on their heads set off
The orchestra of children
Long waiting for their mothers
 "Mama oyo yo, Mama oyo yo"

As the women crossed path
With a war wearied battalion
Of Fed soldiers entering Omoku
The day's song was killed
But God's hand saved the day
From the sorrowful rain of blood

For the women listened
To the native voice
The soldiers' interpreter and guide
 "Don't run, don't run"
The lone voice at the dark moment
Turned the night to day

The guns positioned to kill
Received not the order to shoot
Instead a new song was born
The pass word for life
The victory song…

"One Nigeria, one Nigeria"
Visibly shaken with loads sitting
On their heads; babies strapped
To their backs for some of the women
They returned alive with a new song
To the waiting orchestra
"Mama oyo yo, Mama oyo yo"

*__Mama oyo yo__ (*Children's enthusiastic thrill at seeing their mother return from mart or farm.*)

*__Omoku,__ in the last days of the Nigerian civil war (1970)

BIAFRA

I sing today of Biafra
As a child, who survived
One of the bloodiest chapters
Of the Nigeria story
Pages we cannot close
And pretend it never happened
And carry on with our song
Of *One Nigeria*

I sing today of the children
Killed as child soldiers
Killed at cross fires
Starved to death
The lost generation
Those that became orphans
And lost the childhood experience
Like the Soweto children

I sing today of those pages
Of the Nigeria story
Crying for revisit to make right
All the wrongs done by all sides

Obi   Udo
    Kunle   Inemo
       Tonye   Lalong
              Osaro
              Lugard
              Elechi
       Bello   Obaseki
  Musa   Omoruyi
As we carry on with our song
Of *One Nigeria*
I sing today of Biafra
More than a name
The deep wound bandaged
The bleeding may have stopped
But, the wound needs to heal
So that relief can come
For all to sing joyfully
One Nigeria

I AM JUST A POET

I sing of savages
That have taken over Omoku
Predatory birds
That hover over the homestead
For our chickens
While I sing of their escapade
I sing my song of escape

Where I have just buried
My mother, a man appeared
Wielding a machine gun; orders me
"Oga, make you follow me"
Standing my ground
As a tree on the path of a wind
God's invisible hands saved
The day, giving me a song

I am not your target
The money bags you hunt
Day and night for ransom
I am just a poet
Caught up in the storm
That left me heart broken
With a mouth full of songs

BAGHDAD'S MISERY DANCE

The hellish reality show ended
As abruptly as it had started
Robbing the internet surfers
And TV viewers a pastime

While the sane world was saved
The horrors of war and misery
Stream into their homes
To feed a war-hungry world

Incensed by Saddam's song
 "Mother of all wars"
The world was thrown to war
But, before the watching world
Bagdad fell before the drum beats peaked

ALONE WITH HER GOD

ALI OGBA, I AM BACK HOME

Ali ogba, I am back home
The explorer returns home
Heeds the earth's call
And returns to the sweet home
As an eagle, perched on the Iroko

Ali ogba, I am back home
With my feet on your soil again
There is no better place to alight
And sing this song close to my heart
After traveling across the Atlantic

Ali ogba, I am back home
To sing at the dust return rite
The Holy book orders every roving man
As I return the remains of my mother
To the place her journey started

Ali ogba (Ogba land)

LET MY TEARS FLOW

Let my tears flow like a crying child's
For the day sneaks on everyone
When sons and daughters will cry
Betraying our frailty

Let my tears flow like the River Niger
On my face, as I bewail my mother
The mama whose breast fed me
And hands bathed me

Let my tears flow, like the rain of tears
As at Lazarus' demise
My Lord wept; and the people
Said, "How He loved him"

WHEN A MAN CRIES

By the rivers of Michigan
Far from the Orashi River
Lo, there we heard the news
And we wept like babies

When a man cries like a baby
The naive calls it weakness
Tell me about it, I have been there
Only real men cry like babies

Few are the things that break
The man; making him cry like a baby
For my beloved mother
I cried unashamed like a baby

- **Orashi River** (a tributary of the Niger Delta , in Nigeria)

ALONE WITH HER GOD

She who I have known
All my life, but now cannot
Reach. As I got to town
I entered her room
But her presence was not
Lost, even in her absence

My eyes caught her Bible
By the bed-side table
The Holy book's wear and tear
Spoke volume of her time
Alone with her God
Away from all that distracts

Pics of her grand children
On the wall of the room
Hold your attention like an album
This was her prayer corner
Away from the eyes of the world
Here she sought her God

I left her room
Organized as I found it
Speechless like a child again
Troubled that she was gone
Aware this is one journey
Everyone will take someday

I CANNOT STOP SEEING HER

I cannot stop seeing her
Who stepped out of my life
Without a parting word

I cannot stop wondering
Why her sun set so soon
With many unanswered questions

I cannot stop hoping
I will wake up and see her
Who's gone on a long journey

I cannot stop being the son
Who will always remember her
And thank God, I am her son

I CALLED HER CEE

We called her Cee
The child's first word
For mama
That we never let go

We called her Cee
She was our love
Now we cannot see
Nor reach our love

Now that mama is gone
I cannot see her
Whom I love
And called Cee

OIL SONGS

ABUJA

The capital city built
Overnight with the oil wealth

Sliced like bread
To the highest bidders

Squeezed dry like orange
By political prostitutes

Flooded by the hungry
Seeking a piece of the cake

Stripped of her essence
Like other cities before her

OMOKU

Once a little town
Where under the sun
Everyone knew their neighbors

Once a little town
We joyfully called home
And unashamedly bathe at her streams

Once a beacon of tradition
Now cozy in garment of modernity
With creepy shadows

Today she sprouts under the sun
Burdened and troubled in the mart
Like other oil towns

JOS

Go tell it on Shere hills
And over the land troubled
Sing of her seasonal unjust fires

Angry fires that devastate
Kill and leave colossal waste
In its trail and rising smoke

Sing of the same political hands
Baptizing the town again and again
With fire for their own gain

Sing of the people's throe
Going through seasons of fire
No one or the land benefited from

- **Shere hills** (hills to the East of Jos, capital of Plateau State, Nigeria)

THE OIL PLIGHT

The plight of the Niger Delta
The song no one wants to hear
That haunts her sons, like the curse
The tortoise carry's on its back

Where voices are silenced
Men are declared public enemies
Pitched to cut each other's throat
By the striving tribe of oil thieves

The unjust reality on the ground
And disappointing sell outs
Trail me like the disturbing headache
That emanates from an unfinished task

WE ARE A PEOPLE NOT AFRAID TO STAND

We are a people not great in number
Yet not afraid to take our stand
And raise our voices to be heard

We are a people in the unjust land
Whose hands have been made strong
By our God who bequeathed us the land

We are a people not afraid to stand
Our ground against the oil thieves
And if needed be defend our heritage

We are a people facing environmental war
And they that want us extinct before dawn
Require us to obediently kiss the flag

THE SEASON OF KILLINGS
(For Obi, Ken, Harry, and Dikibo)

I sing of the season of killings
Driven by wild taste for oil and power
We have inherited, while men
Eat, drink, and go to bed

I sing of the cruel killing of Obi
Butchered and dismembered
In his bedroom; and no dust
Was raised in the home front

I sing of the gruesome hanging
Of ken and the Ogoni eight
The voice they could not silence
In the Niger Delta divided tongue

I sing of the murderous hands
That snatched Harry hurriedly out
Of the political landscape
Leaving us with scary nights

I sing of the bloody hands
That took the life of Dikibo
Killers with blood dripping hands
Parading as sons of the soil

I sing of the looming evil day
Generals turned politicians fear
To see in their life time
If this season of killings continue

- **Dr. Obi Wali** (renowned literary scholar, Nigerian statesman, politician and Ikwerre leader).
- **Kenule Saro- Wiwa**(Nigerian writer, Environmental activist and Ogoni leader)
- **Dr. Marshall Sokari Harry**(prominent Nigerian politician and statesman from Degema)
- **Aminasori Kala Dikibo** (prominent Nigerian politician and statesman from Okrika)

THE BROKEN PIECES FALL IN PLACE

GRASS BAPTISM

Walking down the street
These friends look like
A perfect match, save
One uses his eyes, while
The other leads with his nose

Like one on mine search
He stops and snoops
Then raises one leg in the air
To water fire hydrants or
Baptizes the grass

Wait and see him
Stoop to do his business
To cover up his act, he throws
Soil and grass up with his hind legs
Like someone sowing seeds

THE PRODIGAL PATH

Torrent of voices assail us
Every day from without
And within as bullets

'Sun, stand still' Joshua cried
The flaming ball stood
Radiating daylight

'Son, stand still' the man cries
Today, but with ears to hear
He chooses to rebel

As voices beg to be heard
The world awaits the son
With ears to hear

THE BROKEN PIECES FALL IN PLACE

The train stopped
At Chicago's Thorndale station
And a man darts off the couch
Dashed through stairs
And cuts through the exit doors
Into the street like a deer

After his disappearance
Squad cars like attacking bees
Swarmed the station
Letting out men in blue, who ask
Questions and combed the alley
For pieces of the puzzle

Only then did the broken pieces
Drop and fall in place
The scream
The flight
And the wailing
The pick pocket's escape

SONGS OF THE DRUNKEN

For the fallen tree the women
Cried their eyes to virtual dryness
So did the tale bearers of the land

The men gathered more subdued
Like a rain cloud. Their turn out was huge
So did the drunks of the land

The songs of the drunken become
Loud as men sing the dirge
Of the one gone before them

At such ground mortals pour praises
Like rain with gin washed mouths
And their tongues are loosen

THE PAY DAY CURSE

He staggers to the left and a little to the right
Crab-like; as he peers through the dark streets
Of Port Harcourt on his torturous walk home

Each bold step forward was like a toddler's
Giant leap from belly to feet to take
Or catch up with the world fleeing before him

He drank to drown his woes, weighing him
Down, like the carapace the tortoise
Have learned to live with as his armor

With eyes begging to be shot for the day
He walks, like combing through a field
Of elephant grass, a victim of pay day curse

LOST SONG

The verse flourished
Like a lush plant
Sprouting to life
Second by second
The foliage and branches
Deferring gravity
Attempting to kiss the sun
And the gardener came
Pruning here and there
But which touch marred
The plant, I cannot tell
And the song is lost, unsung

MADE IN BANGLADESHI

Far away in Bangladeshi
A sweatshop collapses
Killing hundreds of workers

Far away in Karachi
Hungry and angry flames roast
Hundreds of sweatshop workers

While the rubbles of Bangladeshi
Trapped alive the dying
Who sang buried alive

The grave cry
Of Bangladeshi and Karachi
Seems distant to the West

But the shirt on my back
Cries out in protest
'Made in Bangladeshi'

DOING THE NUMBERS

Our days in this wilderness
from the crib to the grave
are all numbered

A dance of spiral waves
of opposing up and down days
that are swallowed by years

The years are swallowed
into the endless stream of numbers
that define the visible world

ANOTHER MAN'S SHIT
(*General Hospital, Port Harcourt*)

"Here is the sample, madam"
Handing out the lab test tube
Of the requested shit

The frowning nurse looked away
And cries out, "you should have come
With a bucket"

Nobody wants to touch another
Man's shit, like the night soil man
Who wears a mask to avoid recognition

Shit stinks, but shit business
Anywhere any day is good business
Not surprised, she wants an elephant scoop

THE MOMENT OF DISCOVERY

The visit to the gallery
Was to be an escape
From the blistering summer day
As she and her peers bonded
To extend their frontiers
As art lovers

The moment of discovery
Suddenly came as a thief
Face to face with her fear
Alas, a god from her village
Asleep on a stance at the gallery
In the land of Lincoln

Among the sea of art lovers
The African in her, tells her
She's has broken a taboo
Fear from no where enveloped
Her like one exposed
To Chicago's unfriendly cold

So much ado for a god
With mouth, but cannot speak
Has hands, but could not resist
The hands that stole and sold it
While it slept in the land
Where natives revered it

POOR CREATURES

The poor sees he is poor
When he sees the rich
Of the present world

The rich sees he is poor
When he comes to the door
For with nothing we all go back

We are poor creatures
Who should see ourselves
As creatures of our God

BLACK HISTORY MONTH

February every year
They talk of Black history
I sing his story

All year long
They talk of his past
I sing of his present

On their canvas
They paint him black
I sing his song

WATCH AND PREY

When you think we are done
With gallows, man re-invents
The art of strangling himself
And politely calls it neck tie

When you think we should know
How to clothe ourselves; man tightens
The noose around his mid section
And calls it a belt

While the world around him
Is changing, the man
Goggles up like the old owl
To watch and prey

TELLING TALL TALES

PIGEON MAN OF LINCOLN SQUARE
(For Joseph F. Zeman Jr.)

I sing of you today
I sing of your large heart
That made pigeons flock
To your feet to feast at the corner
Where Western and Lawrence streets
Crossed path to let the pigeons coo

I sing of you today
Because of you, the pigeons flap
And cover the sky over Lincoln square
Here curious pigeon followers
Come to watch the air shows
And feed the pigeons

I sing of you today
The man who for pigeons
Broke the law again and again
To let pigeons coo and mate
Unafraid in the city that decreed
"Do not feed pigeons, $500 fine"

I sing of you today
The man pigeons idolized
They perched all over you, to feast
While you stood with outstretched

Hands; a public exhibition that
Appeared and disappeared in a flash
Like the unpredictable Chicago weather

SALUTE TO BARAS
(For Baras Orugbani)

The dazzling star of Port Harcourt
Who graced the grass tuft
Far from the West where
Heroes are lauded and die not

The shooting star shone
As the eagle effortlessly soars
But his sun went down
When his play days were over

He that once charmed the city
Became a shadow of the past
While the West flies the kite of heroism
Our sky has no place for such travesty

- **Baras Orugbani** a former football player of Port Harcourt Sharks club, who was the team's striker and leading goal scorer in the 80s.

A SEASON WITH AKE
(*For Claude Ake*)

I sing of the Choba days
When excellence walked
And students hungered for her
The season he walked
Not only as a son of the soil
But a distinguished professor

He stood tall among his peers
Well liked by hungry students
Whom he fed with his ideology
Sandwiched in his lectures
Like sugar ants, students filled
His lectures for more

We were never disappointed
Drinking from his well
Were autographing in our star
Many would have his brand
To celebrate this famine season
Of academic excellence

As I sing this dirge
The sky of Lagos weeps
To this day the crash
Of Ake's plane into the Lagoon

What giant of a man
The sea swallowed in the crash

Claude Ake (Nigerian professor of Political science, at University of Port Harcourt, who died in a plane crash in November 7, 1996).

POOR OLD OSSIE

The day comes when the boiling pot
Meets the stray fowl, and the wary chant

'Ossie has done it again'
'Ossie has stolen a fowl'

Its a day of shame, when ranting ants
Trail Old Ossie pelting him with curses

'Ossie has done it again'
'Ossie has stolen a fowl'

Like daylight litters of feather tell
Undeniably tales that stir the chant

'Ossie has done it again'
'Ossie has stolen a fowl'

WHAT WE MAY NEVER KNOW OF THAT DARK NIGHT

What the tale bearing mosquito would never know
Was what hit him dead, leaving such a bloody mess

What the sleeping man would never know
Was what the tale the mosquito had for him that night

What we may never know of that dark inglorious night
Was why the serenity of that night was killed for a tale

TELL TALL TALES

The con blames the devil for all his woes
Telling tales to save his neck like a canary

The madman all day talks to himself, for no one
Takes him seriously save his dogging shadow

The drunk spits out everything to your face
Even things that should not see the sun

The mosquito seeks unsuspecting ear
To whisper its presence and tell tall tales

NO WOMAN, NO CRY
(For Little O)

The pain no mother
No woman, should bear
Helplessly watch her baby die
After the joy of celebrating life
Her crying was heard

In the night of her crying
She refused to be comforted
'No woman, don't cry'
Weeping for her son
For he was no more

The weeping shattered
The night's stillness in D/line
Disbelieve hung in the air
Her son violently snatched
By a cooking gas explosion

Far from a war zone
The family's single room haven
That served as the sitting room
Kitchen and bed room
Became the time bomb

- **D/line** (a precinct of Port Harcourt)

AN ODE TO VICTORIA

The beat of drums send the waves clapping
While the people sleep in a land fast receding

As the Atlantic rails in lust, raveling kisses
And caresses the land the people look away

Day after day the sea rails, yet the people pour
Into the beach, mimicking the birds that flew across the sea

Nonetheless at the love nest, the Aladuras seek the way
And as the people celebrate dazzling castles spring to live

- **Aladuras**(a religious sect that dress in white garment and conduct their worship by sea front)

WHAT TALE WOULD YOU TELL?

Here is the hour
The long expected hour
Tween dawn and dusk
A long labor you have to overcome
Like the expectant mother
For you have a promise to keep

Here is the wind
Forerunner of the late rain
Though dried leaves fall
Stand for your calling
Like soldiers, you shall conquer
For you have a promise to keep

Do remember the promise
As your name
A long way, you have come
When the wind stills
And a new dawn reels
What tale would you tell?

(Government Girls Secondary School, Oromenike class of 1991)

A RIVER TO CROSS

Many rivers you have crossed
Many still lie ahead
In the race to be a WOMAN
As if it were yesterday
A six year journey
Has come to an end
Still away lies the land
For there is a river to cross
Farewell, as you row across
As your sun goes down
Remember   God…
And like your mother
Remember your alma mater

(Government Girls Secondary School, Oromenike class of 1991)

82

AS YOUR SUN SETS

As minutes tick away
Hours fly like the eagle
And before you is the day
The long expected day
What would be your song?

As the day grows long
Would your sweet song
Like the time change?
A long way you have come
Remember to hold your peace
For victory lies behind the cloud

As your sun sets
The world leaps to snatch you
What would be your song?
What tale would morrow break?
Just remember God
In Him you will find peace

(Government Girls Secondary School, Oromenike, class of 1992)

MADAM WAS THE MAN

Riding the transit bus
Exposes the bus riders
To an avalanche of the bus
Conductor's unsavory tongue
This ride was different
Madam was the man

Gorgeously and colorfully attired
 In her George-wrappers
With a matching blouse
The drama unfolded like a play
As the bus pulled up
At a crowded PH bus stop

Madam lost her balance
Making her way out of the bowel
Of the bus; triggering a staggered dance
That rocked a man to bawl
"Madam, you want knock me down?"

The protest came against a wall
Madam was in a different world
Like someone in front of the mirror
She was adjusting her wrapper
Coming out with a razor tongue
She slashed, "Na me say make
Your leg no strong for ground?"

-     "Is it my fault that your feet are not firm on the ground?"

Printed in the United States
By Bookmasters